iMath
Readers

Football Numbers:
Graphing Data

by John Perritano

Content Consultant
David T. Hughes
Mathematics Curriculum Specialist

NORWOOD HOUSE PRESS
Chicago, IL

Norwood House Press
PO Box 316598
Chicago, IL 60631

For information regarding Norwood House Press, please visit our website at
www.norwoodhousepress.com or call 866-565-2900.

Special thanks to: Heidi Doyle
Production Management: Six Red Marbles
Editors: Linda Bullock and Kendra Muntz
Printed in Heshan City, Guangdong, China. 208N—012013

Library of Congress Cataloging-in-Publication Data

Perritano, John.

   Football numbers: graphing data / by John Perritano; content consultant,
   David Hughes.
   p. cm.—(iMath)

   Audience: 8–10.
   Audience: Grade 4 to 6.
   Summary: "The mathematical concept of graphing data sets is introduced
   while discussing the sport of football. Readers learn to graph and interpret
   data sets in data tables, bar graphs, picture graphs, and line plots.
   Concepts include intervals and solving 'how many more or less' bar graph
   problems. This book features a discover activity, history connection, and
   mathematical vocabulary introduction"—Provided by publisher.

Includes bibliographical references and index.

ISBN: 978-1-59953-566-1 (library edition: alk. paper)
ISBN: 978-1-60357-535-5 (ebook)

1. Graphic methods—Juvenile literature.
2. Mathematics—Study and teaching (Elementary)
3. Football—Juvenile literature. I. Title.

QA166.P47 2012
001.4'226—dc23
2012035767

CONTENTS

Note to Caregivers:

Throughout this book, many questions are posed to the reader. Some are open-ended and ask what the reader thinks. Discuss these questions with your child and guide him or her in thinking through the possible answers and outcomes. There are also questions posed which have a specific answer. Encourage your child to read through the text to determine the correct answer. Most importantly, encourage answers grounded in reality while also allowing imaginations to soar. Information to help support you as you share the book with your child is provided in the back in the **Additional Notes** section.

Bold words are defined in the glossary in the back of the book.

Tick, Tock

New York Giants **quarterback**, or leader, Eli Manning marched his team down the field. Several New England Patriots ran to **tackle** him. To tackle is to bring a player to the ground. Manning had just enough time to throw the ball to his teammate, David Tyree. Tyree reached into the air. He pinned the ball on his helmet with one hand. He held onto the ball.

The Giants were still alive. They were only 25 yards from the goal line. A **touchdown** was waiting. It would be worth six points. There were only 35 seconds left in the game. *Tick, Tock.* Manning threw a long pass. Plaxico Burress caught it. He crossed the goal line.

Touchdown!

But the Patriots got the ball back. Quarterback Tom Brady threw a pass to Randy Moss. The ball fell to the ground. It was an **incomplete pass**. The crowd went crazy. The Giants had won Super Bowl XLVI!

5

Show the Data

Millions of fans watch football. Many fans collect information, or **data**, about the game. They study players, plays, and scores.

Others collect data about coaches or the fans themselves. They may track how many fans buy tickets to watch games. Or, they may track how often people watch football on television.

Graphs represent, or show, data. Graphs make it easier to read data. They also make it easier to compare data and ask questions.

Idea 1: Data can be represented in a **bar graph**. Look at this example. Numbers are represented in a table. Then, those numbers are represented in a bar graph.

	Number of Touchdowns in One Season				
	46	39	29	45	31
Quarterback	A	B	C	D	E

The graph uses **intervals** of 10 to mark the number of touchdowns. That means each block segment of 10 in a bar equals 10 touchdowns.

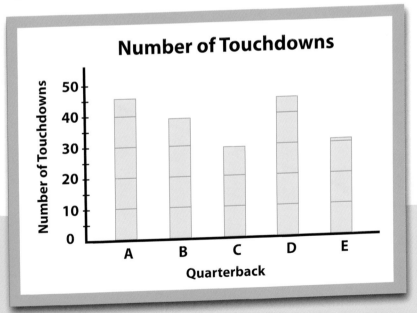

Is representing data in a bar graph a good way to interpret data?

Idea 2: The same data can be represented in a **picture graph**. A picture graph includes a **key**. A key explains the meaning of the pictures in a picture graph. In this picture graph, one football equals 10 touchdowns.

Quarterback	Number of Touchdowns in One Season				
	46	39	29	45	31
	A	B	C	D	E

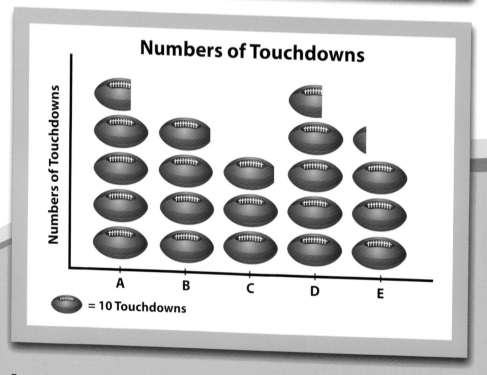

Numbers of Touchdowns

= 10 Touchdowns

Is representing data in a picture graph a good way to interpret data?

Idea 3: Data can also be represented in a **line plot**. For example, this table shows how many hours students played football on a weekend.

Student	Hours
Jack	$2\frac{1}{2}$
Tanisha	4
Laurie	3
Juan	3
Luca	$5\frac{1}{4}$

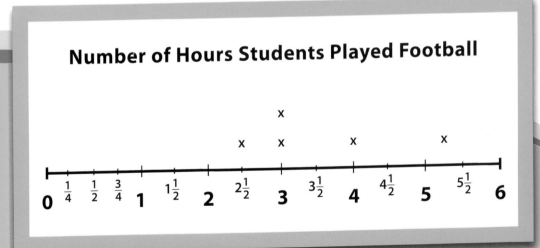

Is representing data in a line plot a good way to interpret data?

DISCOVER ACTIVITY

Materials
- paper
- pencil
- colorful objects

Color Graph

Collect a set of colorful objects. They might be plastic balls. Or they might be marbles or paper clips.

Sort the objects by color. Then, draw a table like the one below. List the objects you have sorted.

Next, count the objects in each pile. Write the number in the table.

The table below is an example of the kind of table you will make.

Object	Number
Red balls	9
Yellow balls	7
Green balls	12

Think about the data in your table. How can you show the data? How can you make the data easier to read? Will you represent the data in a:

- bar graph?
- picture graph?
- line plot?

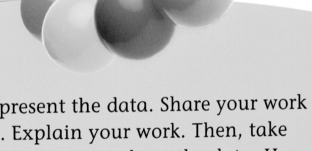

Choose one way to represent the data. Share your work with a friend or adult. Explain your work. Then, take turns asking each other questions about the data. Here are some examples:

- How many different colors of objects are there?
- What do I have the most of?
- What do I have the least of?
- How many more red objects than blue objects are there?

Choose another way to represent your data. Share and explain your work again.

Too Rough for Play

When football was first played in the United States, players did not pass the ball to one another. Players could only kick the ball or pick it up and run with it. The game was rough. Players punched, pushed, and kicked each other. Yet they didn't wear helmets or shoulder pads.

Many colleges found football to be too rough. They wouldn't let students play the game. Too many players got hurt.

But the 26th president of the United States liked football. Theodore Roosevelt wanted to save the game of football and make it safer to play.

Theodore Roosevelt served as President of the United States from 1901 to 1909.

President Roosevelt asked the colleges to make some new rules and to keep playing football. In December 1905, officials met to rewrite the rules so students could play the game again. Until then, players only ran with the ball. They never passed it. But that changed in 1906. The score was 0–0 in a game between two schools. They were Carroll College and St. Louis University. The coach for the St. Louis team did some fast thinking.

Early football players had to learn to play by new rules. One of those rules allowed players to pass a ball through the air.

His team had practiced passing for weeks. So, he told them to start an "air attack." Bradbury Robinson tossed the first forward pass in history. He threw the ball to teammate Jack Schneider. The first pass was incomplete. But Schneider caught the second one. He made a touchdown. St. Louis made several more passes. They won 22–0.

Imagine a team playing in 1906. The bar graph below shows the number of passes players made in five games.

1. What do you notice about the change in the number of passes as the team continues to play games?

2. What is the difference between the least and the most number of passes the team tried?

Being allowed to throw passes was a new rule for football in the early 1900s.

3. Imagine the team played another game. Would you expect the number of passes they tried to go up? go down? stay the same? Why?

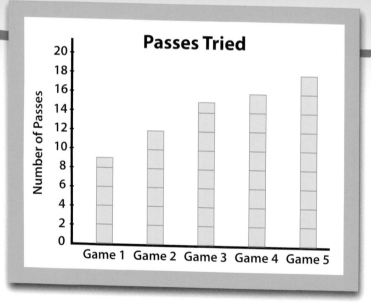

Passes Tried

Number of Passes

20
18
16
14
12
10
8
6
4
2
0

Game 1 Game 2 Game 3 Game 4 Game 5

"Pop" Warner

Glenn Scobey "Pop" Warner coached football for 44 years. He built winning teams wherever he worked. Warner taught players how to make a football spin after a kick. He taught them ways to pass a football.

Read this picture graph. It shows how many passes one of Warner's teams made in five games.

1. How many more passes did the team make in Game 5 than in Game 1?

2. Will the team pass the ball more or fewer times in the next game? Use data to help you decide.

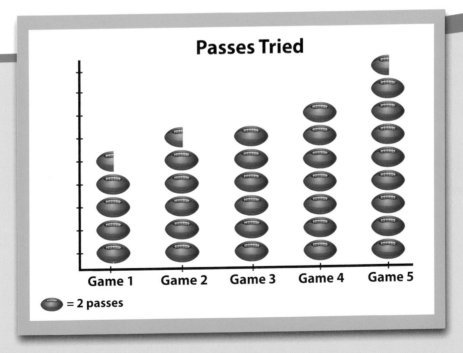

Passes Tried

Game 1   Game 2   Game 3   Game 4   Game 5

= 2 passes

The Rules Change

The rule that let players pass the football changed the game. Officials changed more rules, too. Officials stopped players from locking arms to clear the way for the ball carriers. The length of the game was also shortened. These and other rules made it easier for teams to pass the football.

Football's popularity soared. In 1920, teams from four states met to create the American Professional Football Association. Two years later, the group changed its name. They became the National Football League, or NFL.

In the 1920s, the number of football fans began booming.

Did You Know?

When the NFL first formed, it had 18 teams. Today, there are 32 teams.

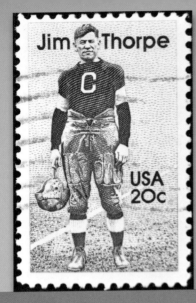

Jim Thorpe was a professional athlete and an Olympic gold medal winner.

Connecting to History

Jim Thorpe was the first president of the American Professional Football Association. Thorpe began his own football career at a college in Pennsylvania. The college was for Native American students. It was there that Thorpe played football for Coach "Pop" Warner.

In 1912, Thorpe played in the Summer Olympic Games in Stockholm, Sweden. He won gold medals in **track and field** events and set records that lasted for a very long time.

Thorpe played both professional baseball and professional football in his athletic career. In 1950, Thorpe won two honors: he was named both the Greatest American Football Player and the Greatest Male Athlete.

The Big Game

In 1925, something amazing happened. About 36,000 fans showed up to watch an NFL Thanksgiving game. It was between the Chicago Bears and the Chicago Cardinals. Professional football had never had so many fans before.

Let's say a coach counted the number of fans who came to watch his team play four games. He used a bar graph to represent the data.

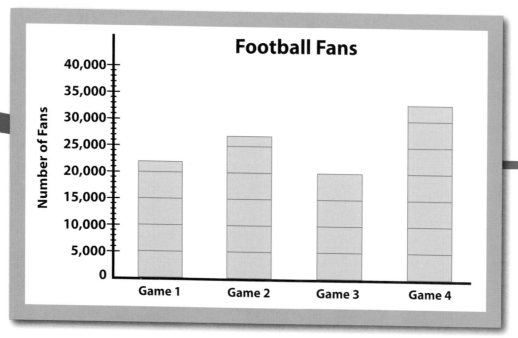

1. What was the least number of fans at a game?

2. What was the greatest number of fans at a game?

3. How many more fans watched Game 4 than Game 3?

Offense and Defense

Playing football today is not what it used to be. The game is much harder. In today's game, which member of a football team is the most important? Some fans would say the quarterback.

The quarterback is like a general. He leads the team. He directs the **offense**. The offense is the team that has the football. It's their job to score points. They must get the ball inside the other team's **end zone**. There are two end zones. They are on opposite sides of the football field.

Quarterbacks are always under attack from opposing players.

The other team is the **defense**. They want to keep the offense away from their end zone.

Sometimes, the quarterback hangs onto the ball. He runs to the goal line himself. At other times, he passes the ball to **receivers**. Receivers catch the pass and run.

Running Backs

A **running back** is also important to offense. The running back runs with the football.

Jim Brown may be one of the greatest running backs of all time. Brown played for the Cleveland Browns for eight years. He started playing in 1957. It was hard to tackle Brown. He was tall. He was heavy. He was strong.

This is the Cleveland Browns Stadium in Cleveland, Ohio.

In his career, Brown ran 14,811 yards of offense. That turned out to be about 104 yards per game. Brown ran for 106 touchdowns and made 126 touchdowns himself.

In 1971, Jim Brown became part of the Pro Football Hall of Fame.

Running backs run toward the other team's end zone. Players for the defense try to stop them. They try to tackle the running back.

This line plot shows the number of yards one team's running backs gained in a game.

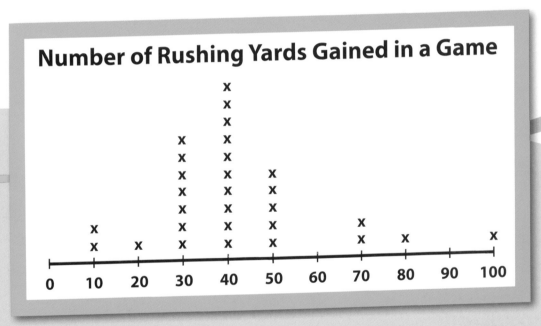

1. How many yards do most running backs gain before they are tackled in a game?
2. Did more running backs run fewer than or greater than 40 yards per game?
3. What is the difference between the most yards run per game and the least yards run per game?

Defensive Linemen

Defensive linemen have a big job to do. Their job is to tackle the ball carrier. They have to be ready to tackle players who get in the way. These players are usually tall and large. Most of them are over six feet tall. They usually weigh about 300 pounds.

Sometimes, defensive linemen tackle a player with the help of other players. Sometimes, they do it alone, or solo. This bar graph shows the number of solo tackles made by five different defensive linemen in one season.

1. What is the greatest number of tackles a lineman made?

2. How many linemen made more than 100 solo tackles?

3. How many more solo tackles did Lineman C make than Lineman E?

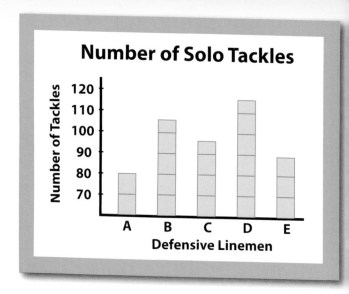

Number of Solo Tackles

Math at Work

Statistics (stuh-TIST-iks) are data. People who collect and study data for a living are called **statisticians** (staa-tih-STISH-uhns). They collect data about large groups of objects or people. Some statisticians work in medicine. Others work for governments. They also work for the environment and for businesses.

Some statisticians collect data about sports. They collect information while watching games. They watch films of the games to check their data. They use the data to understand what's happening. They also use it to predict what will happen in the future.

At the end of a sports season, statisticians summarize their data about players. That's how fans know who runs the most yards or makes the most touchdowns in a football season.

NFL Statistics

At the NFL's website, fans find different kinds of statistics. Some people shorten the word to "stats." People can find stats about their favorite players and teams. They can find weekly news about what outstanding players have done. For example, fans can find out how many touchdowns a player makes in a season.

A referee signals that a player has made a touchdown.

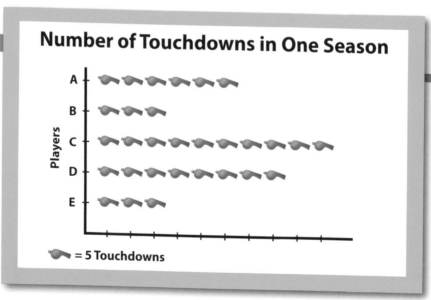

1. Which player had the most touchdowns in one season?

2. How many more touchdowns did Player D make than Player E?

After a team makes a touchdown, it has a chance to win one more point. This point comes from an extra kick.

To score, a kicker must kick the ball through the other team's goal post. This picture graph shows the number of kicks five players made in one season.

This player is holding the ball for a kicker.

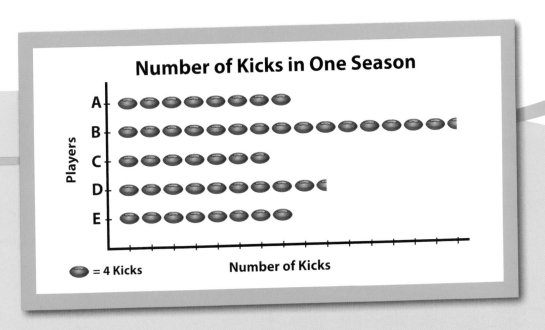

Number of Kicks in One Season

Players

= 4 Kicks   Number of Kicks

1. How many kicks did Player B make in one season?
2. What was the least number of kicks made by these players?
3. How many more kicks did Player B make than Player A?

Going to a Game

Fans of an NFL team may buy a ticket to go watch their favorite team play football. The NFL keeps track of the number of tickets that each team sells for every game. In one year for one team, about 50,000 fans came to each game. That was the least number of fans to see an NFL game live. Another team sold about 85,000 tickets for each game—the most in the league.

Each year, millions of football fans crowd stadiums across the country to watch their favorite teams.

This bar graph represents data for some of the other teams that year.

How many more fans did Team A have than the team that had the second to highest number of fans?

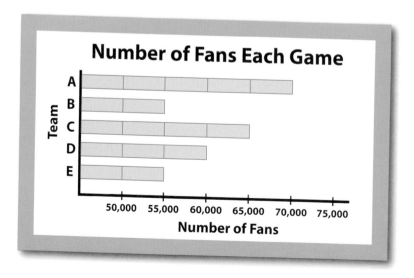

Number of Fans Each Game

iMath IDEAS: Showing Sales

Lots of football fans coming to games usually leads to lots of food sales. Fans buy sodas and popcorn. Hot dogs and pretzels are popular, too.

Food sellers walk up and down the stands during a game. One food seller records her sales in a table.

Food	Hot dogs	Sodas	Popcorn	Pretzels
Total Sold	52	67	44	71

She wants to use a graph to represent the data. That will make the data easier to read and compare. What kind of graph could she use?

Idea 1: She could use a **bar graph**. The food seller sells four different kinds of food. She could choose a number interval that would work best for the numbers she has. Then, she could draw bars to show the number of sales.

Many sports fans enjoy eating pretzels at a game.

Idea 2: The food seller could use a **picture graph**. She would need to choose a picture and make a key to show how many sales each picture represents. This would work, but it could take a long time to draw.

Idea 3: She could use a **line plot** to represent the data. The food seller could write the foods she sold and draw an X above each item to show the total number of sales. This would work, but the line plot will have many X's. That could make the data difficult to interpret quickly.

The seller decides to use a bar graph to represent the data because she can draw this one the fastest. Recreate her bar graph from the data table and then answer these questions:

1. How many more sodas than hot dogs did she sell?

2. Which two foods did she sell the most of?

You can collect other types of data at a football game. That's because football is a game of numbers—the most important of which is the score!

Go team!

WHAT COMES NEXT?

Try collecting your own sports statistics. Go with your family to a game near you. Or watch a game on television. Choose any sport you like, such as soccer, basketball, or softball.

Let's say you choose soccer. Keep track of data in a table. Write the players' names. Keep track of their plays. How many passes do players make? How many times do they kick the ball? How often do they score?

After the game, put your data in a bar or picture graph. Share the graph with friends or an adult. Use the graph to explain the sports statistics you collected. Then, ask the people who saw your graph what they think about it. Use their answers to help you improve your graph.

GLOSSARY

bar graph: a graph that uses bars to represent numbers.

data: information, especially numbers.

defense: players who try to stop the other team from scoring by keeping them out of the end zone.

end zone: a ten-yard area at both ends of a football field.

incomplete pass: a pass that touches the ground before someone can catch the ball.

interval(s): the numbers between two numbers. The interval may or may not include the numbers on either end.

key: an explanation for symbols on a graph.

line plot: a diagram that uses a number line to show the number of times data occur.

offense: players who try to score points by putting a football into the other team's end zone.

picture graph: a graph that uses pictures to represent data.

quarterback: the player in charge of offense.

receiver(s): an offensive player whose job is to catch the ball.

running back: a player on the offense who runs with the ball.

statistician: someone trained to collect and use statistics.

statistics: the study of data, including how to collect it and show it in graphs.

tackle: to bring down an offensive player who's holding the ball.

touchdown(s): a play that scores six points.

track and field event(s): sports that include running, jumping, hurdling, vaulting, and throwing objects such as a javelin.

FURTHER READING

FICTION
The Great Graph Contest, by Loreen Leedy, Holiday House, 2006

NONFICTION
Data, Graphing, and Statistics, by Rebecca Wingard-Nelson, Enslow
    Publishers, 2004
Graphing Sports, by Casey Rand, Heinemann-Raintree, 2010

ADDITIONAL NOTES

The page references below provide answers to questions asked throughout the book. Questions whose answers will vary are not addressed.

Page 14: 1. The number goes up. 2. 9 passes 3. The number of passes would probably go up as players improve.

Page 15: 1. The difference is 8 passes. 2. The team will probably pass the ball more often because the number has increased with each game.

Page 18: 1. 20,000 fans; 2. 33,000 fans; 3. 13,000 more fans

Page 21: 1. 40 yards; 2. fewer than; 3. 90 yards

Page 22: 115 tackles; 2. 2 linemen; 3. 5 tackles

Page 24: 1. Player C; 2. 25 touchdowns

Page 25: 1. 62 kicks; 2. 28 kicks; 3. 30 more kicks

Page 26: 5,000 more fans

Page 28: 1. She sold 15 more sodas than hot dogs. 2. She sold more pretzels and sodas.

INDEX

CONTENT CONSULTANT

David T. Hughes

David is an experienced mathematics teacher, writer, presenter, and adviser. He serves as a consultant for the Partnership for Assessment of Readiness for College and Careers. David has also worked as the Senior Program Coordinator for the Charles A. Dana Center at The University of Texas at Austin and was an editor and contributor for the *Mathematics Standards in the Classroom* series.